# The Southpaw Symphony

## Embracing the Artistry of Left-Handedness

**KING SMARTY**

The Southpaw Symphony

## Table Of Content

# Introduction

Welcome to the enchanting world of left-handedness, where artistry, innovation, and uniqueness converge. "The Southpaw Symphony: Embracing the Artistry of Left-Handedness" is a celebration of the incredible individuals who navigate the world with their left hands and the unparalleled contributions they have made throughout history. As we commemorate International Left-Handed Day, join us on a remarkable journey of discovery and appreciation for the left-handed brilliance that has shaped our world.

# Chapter 1

# A Lefty's World - Unraveling the Enigma

In the vast tapestry of human diversity, left-handedness stands as a mysterious and fascinating thread. In this chapter, we embark on a journey to delve into the captivating world of left-handedness, shedding light on its prevalence, historical significance, and the myths that have enshrouded it for centuries.

Section 1: The Prevalence of Left-Handedness
Left-handedness, though considered a minority, is more common than many might think. We explore the intriguing statistics that reveal the prevalence of left-handed individuals across different cultures and regions. Through scientific research and historical data, we uncover the various factors that might influence handedness, including genetics, prenatal development, and environmental factors.

Section 2: A History of Left-Handedness

From ancient civilizations to modern times, the history of left-handedness weaves a tale of intrigue and complexity. We journey through time to & dddhow left-handedness was perceived in different societies, ranging from admiration to suspicion. Highlighting historical figures who were left-handed, we explore the impact of their contributions on the course of history.

Section 3: Left-Handed Myths and Superstitions
Throughout history, left-handedness has been subject to numerous myths and superstitions, often painting left-handers as sinister or unlucky. We debunk these myths and reveal the truth behind the cultural beliefs that once plagued left-handed individuals. Moreover, we examine the enduring legacy of such superstitions in contemporary culture and how they continue to influence perceptions today.

Section 4: The Southpaw Struggle
In a world designed predominantly for right-handed individuals, left-handers have faced unique challenges. We shed light on the struggles experienced by left-handed individuals in various aspects of life, from using everyday tools and equipment to participating in sports or engaging in artistic pursuits. Despite these challenges,

left-handers have demonstrated resilience and resourcefulness, finding ways to adapt and thrive.

Section 5: Embracing Left-Handed Uniqueness
Rather than viewing left-handedness as a limitation, we explore how left-handers have embraced their uniqueness and turned it into a source of strength. We showcase the stories of left-handed individuals who have harnessed their differences to excel in various fields, demonstrating the power of embracing one's identity to unlock untapped potential.

Section 6: The Rising Voice of Inclusion
In recent times, there has been a growing awareness and advocacy for inclusive environments that accommodate left-handed individuals. We highlight the efforts of organizations, educators, and individuals in promoting inclusivity and providing support to left-handers. This section also showcases the importance of dispelling misconceptions and fostering a culture of acceptance for all handedness types.

Section 7: A Global Celebration of Left-Handedness
International Left-Handed Day serves as a global celebration of left-handed individuals and their contributions to society. We delve into the history

of this commemorative day, its significance, and how it has helped raise awareness about left-handedness worldwide. Furthermore, we explore the events and activities that take place on this special day, uniting left-handers and right-handers alike in celebration of diversity.

Conclusion:
In this captivating chapter, we have embarked on an illuminating journey into the enigmatic world of left-handedness. We have unveiled the prevalence and historical significance of left-handedness, debunked the myths that once cast shadows on this uniqueness, and explored the struggles faced by left-handed individuals in a right-handed dominated world. Most importantly, we have celebrated the resilience and creativity of left-handers, discovering how they have embraced their identity to thrive and make an indelible mark on the world.

As we move forward in this celebration of International Left-Handed Day, let us continue to foster an inclusive society where every individual can flourish, regardless of their handedness. The Southpaw Symphony has only just begun, and its harmonious melody of diversity and acceptance promises to resonate for generations to come.

# Chapter 2

# Left-Handed Greats - Trailblazers and Pioneers

In this awe-inspiring chapter, we pay homage to the left-handed trailblazers and pioneers who have left an indelible mark on various fields, proving that handedness is no barrier to greatness. Their stories serve as a testament to the boundless potential of left-handed creativity and ingenuity.

Section 1: The Artist's Canvas - Leonardo da Vinci
We begin our journey with the iconic Renaissance polymath, Leonardo da Vinci. As a left-handed artist, da Vinci's genius knew no bounds. We delve into the exquisite artworks he crafted with his dominant left hand, demonstrating his exceptional talent in painting, sculpture, and engineering. His innovative ideas and imaginative inventions

continue to inspire generations, revealing the depth of left-handed creativity.

Section 2: A Radiant Mind - Marie Curie
Next, we explore the life and accomplishments of Marie Curie, the pioneering scientist and the first woman to win a Nobel Prize. With her left-handed brilliance, Curie made groundbreaking discoveries in radioactivity, forever altering the landscape of science. Her determination and intellectual prowess serve as a shining example of left-handed excellence in the world of scientific exploration.

Section 3: Triumph on the Court - Rafael Nadal
Turning our attention to the realm of sports, we celebrate the unparalleled talent of Rafael Nadal, a left-handed tennis maestro. Known for his fierce competitiveness and agility, Nadal's success on the court is a testament to the power of left-handed athleticism. His numerous Grand Slam victories and unwavering determination inspire athletes and fans worldwide.

Section 4: A Musical Maestro - Ludwig van Beethoven

In this section, we delve into the world of classical music and the extraordinary contributions of Ludwig van Beethoven. A left-handed pianist and composer, Beethoven's symphonies and sonatas continue to resonate across centuries. We explore how his left-handedness may have influenced his unique musical style and immortalized him as one of the greatest composers of all time.

Section 5: Animated Brilliance - Ned Flanders
In a delightful departure from the historical greats, we celebrate the charm and humor brought to life by Ned Flanders, the lovable left-handed character from the animated series "The Simpsons." As one of television's most iconic left-handed personalities, Ned Flanders showcases the power of creativity in the world of entertainment, captivating audiences with his endearing quirks and memorable catchphrases.

Section 6: Political Visionary - Barack Obama
In the realm of politics, we shine a spotlight on Barack Obama, the 44th President of the United States. As a left-handed leader, Obama's

presidency symbolized hope, change, and progress. We explore the impact of his visionary leadership and the historic achievements that continue to inspire generations.

Section 7: Emerging Left-Handed Talents
In this section, we celebrate the rising stars and emerging talents across various fields, from art and science to sports and beyond. These left-handed individuals are carrying the torch of innovation and creativity, reminding us that the legacy of left-handed greatness is an ever-evolving symphony of brilliance.

Conclusion:
In this chapter, we have journeyed through the annals of history, celebrating the left-handed greats whose achievements have transcended time and space. From the artistic genius of Leonardo da Vinci to the scientific brilliance of Marie Curie, the athletic prowess of Rafael Nadal, the musical maestro Beethoven, the animated charm of Ned Flanders, and the visionary leadership of Barack Obama – each

left-handed pioneer has left an enduring legacy.

The stories of these extraordinary individuals inspire us to embrace our own uniqueness, to harness our creative potential, and to shatter the limitations that society may impose. Their achievements remind us that handedness is but one thread in the rich tapestry of human diversity, and it is the symphony of creativity, talent, and determination that truly defines greatness. As we continue our celebration of International Left-Handed Day, may these remarkable stories kindle the flames of inspiration in the hearts of left-handers and right-handers alike, harmoniously moving forward in pursuit of excellence.

# Chapter 3

# Navigating Adversity - Overcoming Challenges

In this chapter, we delve into the challenges that left-handed individuals encounter in a world primarily designed for right-handed people. Despite the remarkable achievements of left-handed greats, many face hurdles in their daily lives, from using everyday tools to societal misconceptions. However, this chapter also showcases the encouraging strides made by societies and organizations to promote inclusivity and support left-handers, creating a more accommodating and empowering environment.

Section 1: The Struggle of Right-handed Tools
Left-handed individuals often find themselves navigating a world filled with right-handed tools and equipment. We explore the difficulties they encounter when using scissors, can openers, and other gadgets designed for the majority. Through personal anecdotes and research, we shed light on

the frustration that arises when seemingly simple tasks become a challenge due to handedness.

Section 2: Lefties in a Right-handed Classroom
Educational settings can present unique challenges for left-handed students. From the arrangement of classroom desks to the orientation of writing materials, left-handers can feel marginalized in an environment geared towards right-handed learners. We delve into the efforts made by educators and institutions to create inclusive classrooms that cater to the needs of all students, regardless of their handedness.

Section 3: Breaking Stereotypes and Myths
Left-handed individuals have often been subject to myths and stereotypes, ranging from being considered clumsy or awkward to having hidden talents. In this section, we explore the damaging impact of such misconceptions and highlight the importance of dispelling them. By celebrating the achievements of left-handed pioneers and everyday individuals, we aim to reshape societal perceptions and foster a more accepting and supportive atmosphere.

Section 4: Left-Handed Ambidexterity - The Gift of Adaptability

One remarkable aspect of left-handedness is the capacity for ambidexterity, wherein individuals can comfortably use both hands. We explore the unique advantages ambidexterity offers and how it demonstrates the adaptability and versatility of left-handers. Emphasizing the potential of ambidextrous talents, we showcase the achievements of those who have harnessed this gift to excel in various fields.

Section 5: Advancements in Left-Handed Technology

Advancements in technology have paved the way for innovative solutions catering to left-handed individuals. From ergonomic left-handed computer mice to adaptable kitchen utensils, we explore the tools and products that aim to make daily life more accessible for left-handers. Additionally, we recognize the role of technological advancements in creating an inclusive society.

Section 6: Advocacy for Inclusivity

In this section, we highlight the efforts of advocacy groups and organizations dedicated to promoting inclusivity for left-handed individuals. These organizations work tirelessly to raise awareness, challenge stereotypes, and drive positive change in various spheres of life, including education, workplace, and public spaces. By amplifying the voices of left-handers, they foster an environment that celebrates diversity and empowers individuals to embrace their uniqueness.

Section 7: Celebrating Left-Handed Day - A Symbol of Unity
International Left-Handed Day serves as a significant occasion to celebrate the accomplishments and challenges of left-handed individuals worldwide. We explore the events and activities organized on this day, bringing together left-handers and right-handers to appreciate and support the talents and struggles of left-handed individuals alike. The celebration stands as a symbol of unity, fostering an atmosphere of understanding and camaraderie between all members of society.

## Conclusion:
In this enlightening chapter, we have explored the challenges faced by left-handed individuals in a predominantly right-handed world. From the struggles with right-handed tools to the stereotypes and myths surrounding left-handedness, the path to recognition and acceptance has been paved

with obstacles. Nonetheless, we have also witnessed the transformative power of advocacy and technological advancements, which work hand-in-hand to create a more inclusive and accommodating environment for left-handers.

As we celebrate the ingenuity and accomplishments of left-handed individuals, let us remember that each person's unique qualities, regardless of handedness, contribute to the rich diversity that makes humanity thrive. By breaking down barriers and embracing inclusivity, we pave the way for a world where every individual can shine, fostering a symphony of creativity, talent, and unity that resonates for generations to come.

# Chapter 4

# The Southpaw Mind - A Different Perspective

In this illuminating chapter, we delve into the fascinating world of the "southpaw mind," exploring the cognitive differences between left-handed and right-handed individuals. Recent studies have shed light on the unique qualities of the left-handed brain, revealing that diversity in handedness fosters innovation and creativity across various disciplines.

Section 1: The Science of Left-Handedness
We begin by examining the scientific research that has unraveled the complexities of left-handedness. From brain imaging studies to genetic investigations, we explore the neurological and genetic factors that contribute to left-handedness. By understanding the biological underpinnings, we gain insight into the distinct cognitive traits that characterize the southpaw mind.

Section 2: Creativity and Lateral Thinking
One of the hallmarks of the southpaw mind is its propensity for creativity and lateral thinking. We showcase studies that demonstrate how left-handed individuals excel in divergent thinking, problem-solving, and connecting disparate ideas. Their ability to approach challenges from unconventional angles enriches the creative landscape, inspiring innovation in arts, sciences, and beyond.

Section 3: Emotional Intelligence and Empathy
Left-handed individuals often exhibit higher levels of emotional intelligence and empathy. In this section, we explore how the southpaw mind's unique wiring contributes to enhanced emotional awareness and understanding. Their heightened capacity for empathy fosters more profound connections with others, leading to greater cooperation and collaboration in various interpersonal settings.

Section 4: Ambidexterity - A Flexible Advantage
Ambidexterity, the ability to use both hands with ease, is more prevalent among

left-handers. We investigate the cognitive advantages of this trait, including improved coordination, flexibility, and adaptability. Ambidextrous thinkers often thrive in dynamic environments and excel in tasks that require multitasking and quick adaptation to changing situations.

Section 5: Spatial and Artistic Aptitude
Spatial awareness and artistic talent are often pronounced in the southpaw mind. We explore how left-handed individuals demonstrate exceptional skills in fields such as visual arts, architecture, and engineering, where spatial perception is paramount. Their unique perspective and intuitive grasp of spatial relationships contribute to groundbreaking designs and innovations.

Section 6: Academic and Professional Fields Influenced by Southpaw Minds
The left-handed mind's distinct cognitive attributes have a profound impact on various academic and professional fields. We delve into specific disciplines where left-handed individuals have made notable contributions,

such as mathematics, music, design, and psychology. By recognizing and embracing the diversity of cognitive styles, society benefits from a richer and more inclusive array of innovations.

Section 7: Embracing Diversity for a Harmonious Future
In this final section, we emphasize the importance of embracing diversity in handedness and cognitive styles. The symphony of human intellect thrives on the harmonious interplay of different minds, each contributing a unique melody to the grand composition of progress and creativity. By fostering an inclusive environment that celebrates the southpaw mind's unique qualities, we pave the way for a more harmonious and innovative future.

Conclusion:
As we conclude this revelatory chapter, we celebrate the extraordinary cognitive qualities of the southpaw mind. From enhanced creativity and empathy to ambidexterity and spatial aptitude,

left-handed individuals enrich the human experience with their unique perspectives and talents.

The symphony of human intellect is enriched by the harmonious collaboration of diverse minds, each contributing a distinct melody to the grand composition of progress and innovation. By embracing the unique cognitive traits of the southpaw mind, we foster an environment where innovation thrives, creativity flourishes, and humanity takes bold strides towards a brighter and more inclusive future. Let us cherish and celebrate the diversity of the left-handed mind, allowing it to inspire and shape a world that celebrates the creative symphony of all its citizens.

# Chapter 5

# Beyond Handedness - Celebrating Individuality

In this chapter, we transcend the boundaries of handedness and venture into the broader realm of celebrating individuality. While this book has predominantly focused on left-handedness, it is essential to recognize that each person's identity encompasses a multitude of unique qualities that define who they are. We encourage readers to embrace their individuality, respect the diversity within themselves, and cherish the distinctiveness that makes humanity a symphony of remarkable voices.

Section 1: The Tapestry of Human Diversity
Humanity is an intricate tapestry woven from a myriad of experiences, perspectives, and identities. We explore the countless facets that contribute to our individuality, from our interests and passions to our cultural

backgrounds and personality traits. Each thread in this vast tapestry creates a harmonious interplay that defines the beauty of human diversity.

Section 2: Embracing Uniqueness with Confidence
In a world that often pressures individuals to conform to certain norms, this section empowers readers to embrace their uniqueness with confidence. We celebrate the stories of individuals who have overcome societal expectations, letting their authentic selves shine bright. By encouraging self-acceptance, we foster an environment where everyone can flourish, free from the constraints of conformity.

Section 3: The Intersectionality of Identity
Identity is multi-dimensional, and this section explores the intersectionality that enriches our lives. We highlight how various aspects, such as gender, ethnicity, sexuality, and abilities, intersect to form complex and unique identities. Emphasizing the importance of inclusivity, we recognize the power of embracing diverse

identities and experiences to foster empathy and understanding.

Section 4: Nurturing Creativity in All Forms
Just as left-handed individuals exhibit unique creative traits, so too does every individual possess the potential for creativity in their own way. In this section, we celebrate the diverse forms of creativity that manifest in art, science, music, literature, and everyday life. By nurturing creativity in all its expressions, we inspire innovation and progress across myriad disciplines.

Section 5: Building Inclusive Communities
Building upon the theme of inclusivity, this section encourages readers to contribute to the creation of inclusive communities. By fostering environments that celebrate individuality and respect diverse perspectives, we lay the foundation for a harmonious and collaborative society. Inclusive communities empower individuals to embrace their identities and contribute authentically to the collective symphony of life.

Section 6: Empathy and Understanding
Central to celebrating individuality is the practice of empathy and understanding. In this section, we explore the power of listening to each other's stories, acknowledging shared struggles, and appreciating the unique journeys that shape our lives. By cultivating empathy, we forge connections that bridge differences, fostering a sense of unity amidst our individuality.

Section 7: The Symphony of Humanity
As we reach the crescendo of this chapter, we reflect on the symphony of humanity, composed of diverse voices and experiences. The harmonious interplay of our individual melodies creates a symphony that reverberates with resilience, creativity, and compassion. By celebrating our individuality and embracing the uniqueness in others, we weave a masterpiece that defines our shared human experience.

Conclusion:
In this final chapter, we have journeyed beyond handedness and celebrated the beauty of individuality in all its forms. Just

as left-handedness has its unique strengths, so do each of us possess a myriad of qualities that contribute to the rich diversity of humanity. By embracing our individuality, respecting the uniqueness of others, and nurturing creativity and empathy, we create a harmonious symphony that resonates with the essence of life.

As we conclude this book, we extend an invitation to all readers to celebrate their own individuality and appreciate the diverse qualities that make us who we are. Let us remember that in the grand composition of humanity, every voice, every perspective, and every identity matters. May the celebration of individuality continue to enrich our lives, inspire innovation, and build bridges of understanding that unite us as one symphony of humanity.

The Southpaw Symphony

In this symphony of unity, we have traversed the captivating world of left-handedness, celebrated the greatness of left-handed pioneers, explored the challenges faced by left-handers, and embraced the unique cognitive qualities of the southpaw mind. Throughout this journey, one resounding theme echoes: the power of unity and mutual respect between left-handers and right-handers.

As we recognize the diversity of handedness and individuality, we realize that our collective strength lies in embracing our differences. The world becomes a canvas of boundless possibilities when we come together, respecting each other's strengths and perspectives. In this harmonious collaboration, left-handers and right-handers complement each other, contributing their distinct melodies to the grand symphony of humanity.

The celebration of International Left-Handed Day serves as a poignant reminder that diversity is a gift to cherish and a catalyst for progress. By appreciating the unique talents and struggles of left-handers, we cultivate empathy and understanding. In turn, we pave the way for inclusive communities where all individuals, regardless of handedness or any other identity, can thrive and contribute meaningfully.

In this symphony of unity, we acknowledge the importance of advocating for inclusive environments that accommodate the needs of all. From classrooms and workplaces to public spaces, we strive to create an atmosphere that celebrates diversity and fosters collaboration.

As we conclude this heartwarming journey, let us carry forth the melody of unity and respect into the world beyond these pages. Together, let us compose a symphony that embraces the uniqueness of every individual, harmonizing our strengths and perspectives to create a future that celebrates the beauty of human diversity. With left-handers and right-handers together, we create a world that is richer, more vibrant, and full of promise. May this symphony of unity resonate for generations to come.

# Epilogue

# Embracing Diversity in Parenting - Nurturing Left-Handed Brilliance

As we conclude "The Southpaw Symphony: Embracing the Artistry of Left-Handedness," we turn our focus to the parents of left-handed children, offering guidance on nurturing their uniqueness and fostering an inclusive environment. Parenting plays a crucial role in shaping a child's self-esteem, creativity, and resilience. Here are some essential pieces of advice for parents, especially those who may encounter challenges related to left-handedness:

1. Embrace and Celebrate Individuality:
Every child is born with their unique set of talents, strengths, and preferences. As parents, it is essential to celebrate and embrace your child's individuality, including their handedness. Whether left-handed or right-handed, each child has the potential to achieve greatness in their own way.

2.    Avoid    Punishing    or    Discouraging Left-Handedness:
Spanking or punishing a child for being left-handed is not only ineffective but can also be emotionally damaging. Instead, provide a supportive and nurturing environment where your child feels accepted and valued for who they are. Encourage them to use their left hand confidently and explore their creativity without fear of criticism.

3. Create an Inclusive Learning Environment:
If your child attends school, collaborate with their teachers to ensure the classroom is inclusive of all handedness types. Encourage the use of left-handed tools, provide left-handed desks when possible, and advocate for a supportive educational environment where left-handers can thrive academically and creatively.

4. Be Mindful of Language and Stereotypes:
As parents, be mindful of the language you use when discussing left-handedness or any other identity. Avoid perpetuating stereotypes or making negative remarks about being left-handed. Instead, use positive language to celebrate your child's uniqueness and encourage their self-confidence.

5. Provide Left-Handed Tools and Support:
Invest in left-handed tools and equipment, such as left-handed scissors or left-handed notebooks. This simple act shows your child that their needs are respected and valued. Providing them with the right tools can boost their confidence and creativity.

6. Encourage Creative Exploration:
Left-handers often demonstrate a flair for creativity and lateral thinking. Encourage your child to explore their interests and passions, whether in arts, music, sports, or other fields. Support their curiosity and provide opportunities for creative expression.

7. Foster Empathy and Inclusivity:
Teach your child the value of empathy and inclusivity. Encourage them to appreciate diversity in all its forms and to respect the differences in others. By nurturing empathy, you lay the foundation for a kinder and more compassionate world.

8. Be a Role Model for Acceptance:
Lead by example by embracing diversity and inclusivity in your own actions and interactions. Show your child that being open-minded and accepting of others, regardless of handedness or

any other identity, is a fundamental aspect of being a caring and respectful individual.

In conclusion, "The Southpaw Symphony" is not just a tribute to left-handers but a reminder of the power of diversity in shaping a better world. As parents, you have the opportunity to create an environment where your child's unique brilliance can shine. By celebrating their left-handedness and nurturing their individuality, you empower them to dream differently, achieve greatness, and make a lasting impact on the world. Embrace the beauty of diversity and be the conductor of a symphony that celebrates the artistry of every child, including the left-handers who dare to dream differently.

www.ingramcontent.com/pod-product-compliance
Lightning Source LLC
Chambersburg PA
CBHW070118010626
45794CB00013B/2906